Everything You Should Know Perhaps Nothing

A True Story

Volume I

BY: TODD ANDREW ROHRER

iUniverse, Inc.
New York   Bloomington

Everything You Should Know Perhaps Nothing

iUniverse books may be ordered through booksellers or by contacting:

iUniverse
1663 Liberty Drive
Bloomington, IN 47403
www.iuniverse.com
1-800-Authors (1-800-288-4677)

ISBN: 978-1-4401-2411-2 (pbk)
ISBN: 978-1-4401-2412-9 (ebk)

Printed in the United States of America

iUniverse rev. date: 2/3/2009

Every idea in these words is hypothetical.

Every word in these sentences is hypothetical.

You are now able to be in a spirit of open mindedness.

Perhaps it is wise for one to be open minded about things.

Perhaps means maybe.

Do not like these words.

Do not start to like these words.

Do not hate these words.

Do not start to hate these words.

Let the words be.

On the surface these words appear to be wisdom or foolishness.

The deeper meaning of these words is their spirit.

"Do not take the word of a blind man, ask questions."

I dedicate this story and these words to you.

Controversy

1. A **prolonged public dispute**, debate, or contention; disputation concerning a matter of opinion.
2. **contention**, strife, or **argument.**

This is not a story as much as it is an experiment.

It is a prolonged public dispute, contention or argument.

I am certain all will perceive some wisdom in these words.

I perceive wisdom in all of these words.

There is a blanket "perhaps" in front of every word and every sentence in this book.

Attempt to forget that.

Being recognized by an important being is a reward beyond value.

I am pleased you have recognized me by reading these words because you are an important being and

being recognized by an important being is a reward beyond value.

The **Pulitzer Prize** is an American award regarded as the highest national honor in **literary** achievements.

Literature is the **art** of written works. Literally translated, the word means "acquaintance with letters"

Art is the process or product of **deliberately arranging elements** in a way **that appeals to the sense or emotions.**

The Pulitzer Prize in literature is awarded to one who is able to best arrange words in a deliberate fashion in order to make the reader of the words feel the words arranged are appealing ,relating to emotions or senses.

God did a bunch of things but no person has yet determined what God is, they just try to suggest what God is, but they never quite figure out what God is.

So perhaps God is to mysterious, so some men give up trying to determine what God is, and some men deny that there is God, and some men claim they know God .

The men who have given up on determining what God is, perhaps have understood they are unable to determine what God is.

The ones who deny there is a God have perhaps determined it's best to live in denial, than try to understand what God is. Perhaps one can never understand what God is.

The ones who claim they know God are perhaps the most confused, because they perceive they are able to determine what most others have determined, men are not able to determine.

Perhaps God has left enough hints of what God is, so that man is just confused enough to know, man is unable to determine what God is.

Perhaps that toying or trickery or joke if you will, is an indication of who we, humans, are dealing with, as far as who God is.

Perhaps this trickery , if you will, is an indication men are very out classed compared to God, because perhaps Gods trickery is far beyond our understanding at times.

Perhaps this advanced trickery , if you will, is better understood when one understands, God suggested, man's ways are not my ways, Man is unable to understand my ways.

Perhaps God is so trickery or its ways are so advanced, man doesn't stand a chance unless man is in a certain state of mind, relating to understanding Gods ways, so perhaps that is why man has so much difficulty in understanding what God is.

I would like to thank Wikipedia for providing words arranged in a certain fashion so I am able to better understand things.

A **human being**, also **human** or **man**, is a member of a species of bipedal primates in the family Hominidae (taxonomically *Homo sapiens* — **Latin: "wise human" or "knowing human").** DNA evidence indicates that modern humans originated in east Africa **about 200,000 years ago.**

Latin: "wise human" or "knowing human".

Perhaps" wise human" is not as accurate as potentially wise human because I am aware there are perhaps some not so wise decisions being made on this earth by humans, so there are decisions being made on this earth by "potentially wise humans" not "wise humans."

So perhaps 200,000 years ago humans came to be.

"Perhaps" is need because we may discover we came before 200,000 years ago eventually.

As in 250,000 years ago instead of 200,000.

So perhaps works.

"knowing human"

This is perhaps tricky. Knowing suggests other creatures do not know. That's not true.

Knowing is pleasing because it suggests humans know. That suggests humans know something.

I am aware a dog knows something. I am aware a ant knows something. I am aware a human knows something.

Perhaps "Knowing human" is redundant.

Perhaps "Knowing Human" is saying, Humans know they know something other creatures who know something, do not know.

That is perhaps what it is saying, but that is a somewhat flawed way to look at humans.

An eagle can see far better than a human with his sight or vision, so that eagle knows or see's things at a certain distance a human is not able to see, at that distance.

I don't see eagles walking around saying I am a "knowing eagle"

Perhaps eagles did not invent words, because eagles are so advanced they do not have to use words.

Perhaps a man would suggest an eagle is so dumb compared to man.

Perhaps that man is able to fly and able to see vast distances with his vision then.

I am a man and I am not able to fly like an eagle can fly and I am unable to see vast distances with my eye sight like an eagle is able to.

So perhaps it is not wise for me to determine an eagle is not as wise as I am, because that would negate the definition of homo sapiens which is "Wise Human", because suggesting an eagle is not as wise as a human when an eagle is perhaps wiser than a human or as wise as a human would be an unwise conclusion.

Humans can perhaps make tools but so can chimpanzees' and so can perhaps other animals.

Humans can build structures but a bird can build a nest.

Humans can use chemistry but a spider can make web that is as strong as any steel man has ever made and is able to make that web at room temperature when man needs very extreme temperatures and extreme pressures to make his steel, and that steel is still not as light as a spiders fiber is.

Spider silk is a remarkably strong material. Its tensile strength is superior to that of high-grade steel, and as strong as <u>Aramid</u> filaments, such as <u>Twaron</u> or Kevlar. Most importantly, spider silk is extremely lightweight: a strand of spider silk long enough to circle the earth would weigh less than 16 ounces

Perhaps a strand of Kevlar and Aramid or twaron fiber is able to reach around the world and perhaps it would only weight less than 16 ounces, but I am certain we are unable to make it at room temperature and make it within our body as a result of eating food, and I am certain we are unable to use it as food source if we could make it from our own body.

In some cases, spiders may even use silk as a source of food

Perhaps man does not know if a spider was always able to make that fiber.

Perhaps that spider figured out how to enable its self to make that fiber over time.

Perhaps that spider is the" knowing spider" and man is the "one who knows little human."

Perhaps "one who knows little human" knows so little, because "one who knows little human" perceives he knows much.

Perhaps "one who knows little human" should first understand he knows little, so that perhaps then he will know something. Not everything, just something.

Then we can understand we are "knows something human" instead of "one who knows little human" because "wise human" is perhaps not in the ball park as far as accurately describing a human.

Perhaps man should forget everything he is trying to do and spend the next thousand years or so, just trying to figure out why the spider is light years beyond us in nearly every way as far as intelligence, understanding , and abilities. Then perhaps we can suggest we are "slightly wise human".

Perhaps since we do not know how much we know , and since we do not know how much there is to know, we may know nearly nothing compared to how much there is to know.

Perhaps it would be proper to suggest we are "knows nearly nothing human".

My intuition suggests that is a pretty accurate definition for a human.

When an adult suggests a child should go to school, the child perhaps will suggest I do not want to go to school, I would rather stay home and play with my toys.

The child may become upset or sad they are directed to go to school by the adult.

The child may perceive they are suffering. The adult may perceive the child is suffering or being unreasonable.

The adult is certain school is proper for a child to attend, so that child gets educated.

The adult perhaps becomes frustrated with the child because the child is perceived to be acting unreasonable.

The adult perceives the child does not know school is required for proper education, and the adult perceives the child is avoiding school because the child is unaware education is needed to live a proper life.

If one has proper education from going to school one is able to make a proper amount of money and perhaps lead a proper life.

So perhaps a proper life is defined by one who has proper amounts of money.

If leading a proper life is not related to having proper amounts of money then having a proper education from going to school is not needed.

If leading a proper life is related to having a proper amounts of money then perhaps governments should just provide children with proper amounts of money and then they will be able to save money because they will not have to fund so many schools.

Perhaps a proper life is what one determines a proper life is.

Perhaps there is no proper definition of a proper life.

That would enable anyone to define a proper life.

Perhaps if anyone is able to define a proper life that would take power away from ones who attempt to define a proper life.

Perhaps ones who try to define what a proper life is would not be pleased if everyone were able to define what is and what is not because they would understand they have no power.

Perhaps they desire to have power and perhaps they will take care of anyone who tries to take that power away from them.

Perhaps they are unable to let go of their grip on power.

Perhaps their ego is so strong it will not let them let go of their grip on power.

Perhaps they are not meek enough .

Perhaps they are unable to turn the other cheek.

Perhaps they are unable to submit the power they perceive they have and it is causing symptoms like anger and frustration.

Perhaps these symptoms are indications they are willing to do anything at any time to hold onto that power, and that perhaps suggests they are unstable.

Perhaps one who is unstable should not be determining what is the proper way to do things , and one who is unstable should not be suggesting to others what the proper way to do things is.

Perhaps it is not proper for a country to elect officials who are mainly concerned with holding onto power and are willing to do anything to hold onto that power.

Perhaps these officials who are determining the laws for that country are determining laws that keep themselves in power.

Perhaps one may suggest democracy is not perfect but it's the best we have.

Perhaps "it is the best we have" in the past , but perhaps it is not the best we have in the present.

Perhaps one perceives one leader or dictator leads to corruption, and perhaps it does or perhaps history has indicated it does.

Absolute power corrupts absolutely.

This is an indication that ones who have had absolute power have been corrupted in the past.

Power is an emotional desire. Control is an emotional desire.

Love is a form of control. Hate is a form of control.

I am mindful to have no standards but I usually end up with low standards.

When people tell me what I am not, it is frustrating, but when people tell me what I am, it is more frustrating.

The proof is in the pudding.

A drug addict is aware the drug they are addicted to is harmful because they have heard others suggest it is harmful.

The drug addict still uses the drug although he is aware the drug is harmful.

So the drug addict knows the drug is harmful but he doubts it is very harmful.

So the drug addict is in a form of denial.

He knows it makes sense drugs are harmful but he denies drugs are fully harmful.

Because of this denial or confusion he remains an addict.

Once the drug addict is fully aware drugs are fully harmful he quits drugs.

Some drug addicts become fully aware the drug is fully harmful before it is to late.

Some drug addicts do not become fully aware the drug is fully harmful until it is to late, but then it is to late.

Emotions are a drug. Emotions are exactly like a drug and the user exhibits the exact same characteristics as a drug addict does.

When one perceives the sun goes down one perceives it gets dark and they perceive temperature drops.

Perhaps the sun goes down because it gets dark.

Perhaps the temperature goes down, that causes it to get dark and that causes the sun to go down.

Perhaps no man can prove it one way or another.

If a man suggests the heat from the sun goes away when the sun goes down and that causes it to get dark then that man is suggesting absence of light causes darkness.

But pitch black darkness is not real because some creatures at the bottom of the ocean are able to sense quite well in pitch black darkness. If a creature is able to sense in pitch black darkness there must be a form of light and if there is not, then it is pitch black darkness.

The absence of darkness and light is empty space.

The absence of everything is nothing or empty space or a true vacuum.

It perhaps is not possible to have pure light or pure darkness.

It perhaps is not possible to have all of one and all of another.

So some areas appear to have more light than others and some areas appear to have more darkness than others.

Perhaps a blind person is still able to see light because a blind person is unable to see pure darkness.

If one closes their eyes do they see pure darkness or is their flashes of light created in the mind perhaps.

Perhaps the color black in only an indication there is light just a different form of light.

So perhaps there is no darkness there is only light, just varying degrees of light.

So perhaps when the light varies it produces night and the temperature appears to decrease.

The creature at the bottom of the ocean perhaps does not perceive the temperature has decreased because in his form of light the sun going down does not vary the temperature due to the fact he is at depths in the ocean no sun light reaches there to begin with.

So if one asks that creature in the depths ,"Does the temperature decrease when the sun goes down?" he would suggest, "No it does not.", and he would be accurate.

So this creatures perception is accurate and perception is all that creature knows.

So perhaps a humans perception is all a human knows.

Perhaps that is a problem.

If one human perceives there is no time and another human perceives there is time, only a machine that can detect time or detect there is not time can tell who is correct.

Perhaps if a man who creates this time detection machine perceives time he will make that machine so it can detect time and so that machine will detect time.

Perhaps a clock who's hands are moving does not prove there is time, it only prove a man who perceives time made the clock, and that clock gives the man who created it what he wanted, time.

Perhaps if a human perceives there is no time then he will make a clock that does nothing but show there is no time, so he will get what he wanted, no time.

Perhaps humans should not perceive there is time until they first prove there is time.

Perhaps one might argue if there is no time then why do things get older and die, that proves time passes.

Perhaps if one was able to place a creature in a true vacuum or in true empty space it would not die because in a true vacuum there is no time. If there was time in a true vacuum it would not be a true vacuum because a true vacuum is empty space.

One perhaps could argue, science has never been able to detect a true vacuum because nature does not allow a true vacuum or empty space.

Perhaps if one was in a true vacuum or empty space one would not be able to ever detect it because empty space is unable to detect empty space because if it is empty space there is nothing there.

Perhaps if one is nothing one is unable to have something.

Perhaps if one is something then one is unable to have nothing.

If nature will not allow a true vacuum it is because nature is a true vacuum.

If nature is a true vacuum then there is no time because there is nothing in a true vacuum.

If nature is a true vacuum then there is no death because death is something.

So perhaps death is nothing but a perception.

So perhaps life is nothing but a perception.

So perhaps light is nothing but a perception.

So perhaps everything is an illusion because in reality nature is a true vacuum or nothing.

When a physicist tries to understand everything they find more questions .

They prove one theory and that enables ten more theories.

They prove those 10 theories and that enables 100 more theories.

They perceive they are getting somewhere.

They perceive if they can just prove one more theory they will get further along.

But as they get further along they get more theories so they actually go back words because they have more theories to prove than they started with.

So now they have more theories so they have more to know.

They perceive the more theories they prove the more advancement is happening.

But in a true vacuum there is no advancement because there is nothing but empty space.

So we are back to how does one prove reality is not a true vacuum.

There is no way to prove reality is not a true vacuum because reality is a true vacuum.

There is no way to understand everything because there is

nothing to understand.

One cannot understand nothing or there would be something.

So this perception man in general has, is causing problems.

It's causing man to perceive things are there when there is nothing there.

If one perceives there is aliens attacking him, but there is not, one is delusional in their perception.

If one is delusional in their perception one is called delusional.

If one man perceives there is time and one man perceives there is no time, if the judge of who is right is a man who perceives time, he will perceive the man with no sense of time, delusional.

If the two men who perceive time suggest the one who has no sense of time is delusional, that does not prove there is time. That only proves two delusional men are suggesting another delusional man is delusional.

If perception causes creatures who are alive to be delusional in their perception then being alive is causing delusions.

Perhaps being alive is a symptom of being delusional.

Perhaps being delusional is a symptom of being alive.

Perhaps perception one is alive and perception one is delusional is a symptom of perception but that is all.

Being alive and being delusional would not be real in a true vacuum.

In a true vacuum being alive and being delusional would both be illusions.

Perhaps a being who perceives they are alive is symptom that being is delusional.

Man at one time perceived the earth was flat. They were certain and all "normal" men were certain the earth was flat.

Now we understand all the "normal" beings who perceived the earth was flat at that time were delusional beings.

At this point in existence "normal" beings are assuming they can not possibly be delusional, although they are aware a one point all the "normal" beings were delusional.

The scientists today know the scientists long ago were delusional in their belief the earth was flat.

The scientists today know for certain the earth is round.

The scientists long ago were certain the earth was flat.

The name atom comes from the Greek ⷠτομος/átomos, α-τεμνω, which means uncuttable, something that cannot be divided further.

So some being perceived the atom is uncuttable or can not be divided further.

But scientists today understand the atom is indeed cuttable and can be divided further.

An atom bombs explosion is caused by atoms being cut or split.

So now scientists perceive there are many things smaller than atoms.

At one time man could not perceive anything could be smaller than atoms.

So the scientists today are convinced there are things smaller than atoms and they perceive all they have to do is find that one thing than cannot possibly be divided further and cannot be cut further.

They are in search of a thing that is uncuttable and something that cannot be divided further, yet they are aware at one point someone who determined an atom cannot be divided further was delusional in their belief an atom was uncuttable.

Scientists are aware at one point beings believed in things.

Now the scientists perceive the things those beings once believed in were illusions caused by delusional beliefs.

If reality is a true vacuum it is full of illusion and full of beings who believe the illusions are real.

An illusion is nothing. It is not real.

A true vacuum is real but the illusions in it are not real.

Perhaps if reality is a true vacuum and illusions are the only thing in this true vacuum , then illusions are capable of anything because illusions are not real to begin with.

Every being is aware there are illusions.

Some beings are aware of more illusions than other beings.

The being who is fully aware is the being who perceives everything is an illusion.

The being who is not fully aware is the being who

perceives some things are not illusions.

So a being who is fully aware everything is an illusion is not delusional.

A being who is only aware some things are illusions is delusional.

A being who has no sense of time is aware time is an illusion because they are fully aware time is an illusion.

So a being who is aware time is an illusion or has no sense of time is not as delusional.

So a being who has a sense of time is more delusional.

One who perceives no time , has infinite time.

One who perceives time, never has enough time.

"When the going gets weird, the weird go pro."

I am pro.

A woman who perceives they have had a child and has experienced pregnancy, can explain to a man who has never been pregnant and has never had a child, what child birth and being pregnant is like.

This woman can write a million books and write every single detail that happens but that man will never ever know truly what it is like to be pregnant and to have a child.

A **gamma wave** is a pattern of brain waves, associated with perception and consciousness.

So if one adjusts their gamma waves they can perceive differently.

So if one adjusts their gamma waves one being might go from perceiving time to not perceiving time.

So if one adjusts their gamma waves one can have a different sense of consciousness.

Adjusting Gamma Wave patterns does not mean one has to reach abnormal gamma wave patterns.

They are just adjusted from the low end spectrum to the high end spectrum of what is medically considered normal.

Perhaps when I lost my sense of time I also lost my emotional baggage because I perceived I had emotional baggage.

Perhaps the many years of depression this emotional baggage caused me was caused by the illusion emotions.

Perhaps by blocking or denying emotions enough one will adjust their gamma waves to the point they will perceive no emotions and then they will not have any emotional baggage and then they will not have to worry about emotional problems and many psychologists will be out of work and the anti depression medicine companies will have to adjust their marketing strategy.

Perhaps this jesus being arose from the dead for a reason.

He talked much about things.

John 3:16

God so loved the world he gave his only son and whoever believe in him shall not perish but have eternal life.

Let's pretend.

God so loved the world in this true vacuum he gave his only (no sense of time) Son and whoever perceives there is no sense of time shall not die because they will be aware there is no death..

Let's pretend further.

God so loved the world in this true vacuum or empty space, one day in this empty space, a being adjusted their gamma waves, by blocking emotions and ego enough, they had no sense of time. And since this being adjusted their gamma waves, they perceived there was no time, and since they perceived there was no time, they became aware time is an illusion, and since they became aware time was an illusion, they also perceived everything is an illusion, and that made them perceive everything is nothing or a true vacuum, so then they perceived death and life are also an illusion, so they understood it was not possible to die, because death is simply a strong illusion, and anyone who adjusts their gamma waves enough, will also know death is an illusion so they will know they don't die, because death and life are something, and a true vacuum is nothing, so death and life are illusions.

So being upset about someone dying is emotional baggage created by gamma wave perceptions and death is nothing to fear because death is an illusion and fear is an emotion and if one has few emotions they won't have fear.

Everyone is aware God shows itself in many ways.

Look how advanced we are, look at the stars and look at a flower, God does exist.

Yes.

People pray to God and say I felt God when I was near death and I felt God when I prayed.

Yes.

See you are aware of god.

You are just not aware of what god is. Gamma wave adjustments will make you aware of what god is.

God is everything. God created the true vacuum but God is outside the true vacuum.

Nature is a true vacuum.

What is a true vacuum?

Empty Space or nothing.

So with God anything is possible?

Yes.

Why?

Because anything is possible in a true vacuum because anything is a true vacuum is an illusion.

Isn't an illusion something?

No. An illusion is not real. So it can happen in a true vacuum.

So if everything is an illusion there is no purpose?

No. If everything is an illusion we can do anything so we have unlimited purpose.

Why can't one walk on water?

They do not believe they can.

Why?

Because they perceive time and they believe the illusions are real, so they can't get past them.

Can you do anything, now you are aware reality is an illusion?

Yes. I can do things a being with a sense of time will ever be able to accomplish.

What is that, author of these words?

I can arrange these words in a fashion, no being with a sense of time can ever accomplish.

I can arrange words, that give off the illusion called wisdom and I can do it without much effort.

Some beings with a sense of time can write 80 thousand word novels and the last words on the last page of their huge novel has one lesson or one event of wisdom.

It takes 80 thousand words to make one sentence of perceived wisdom.

I would be hard pressed to accomplish so little with so much.

Your guess is as good as mine.

I can tell the truth and not be concerned with what others will say or think because I have almost no emotions or ego. I will not get emotional if someone says this book is wrong, or this book is crap, or this person is unstable by the words they say. I am free of my emotional cage. I am not concerned about what others perceive I am, because I am fully aware of what I am. I am fully aware what others perceive I am, is wrong. What others perceive I am is just an illusion they believe. I am fully aware I am an illusion, emotions are an illusion, time is an illusion. Illusions cannot harm me. One may perceive I am unsafe in my perception, but I am fully aware I have never been safer in my entire life than I am after the 'accident".

Nothing can harm me ever, because I am nothing and so I am very safe. I rely on myself and knowing my self is an illusion. I can live with that. See, the awareness one has when they adjust their gamma waves by blocking emotions for three to six months is so powerful that I am unable to describe how powerful the perception I have is. I can only try. I am aware, a drug addict is not going to openly admit they are a drug addict. The drug addict who admits they are addicted to drugs, has a chance to kick drugs.

The drug addict who does not even admit they are a drug addict has no chance.

So the drug addict who does not admit they are a drug addict is doomed . They are doomed while they are in that denial stage.

So a parent who see's their offspring addicted to drugs, comes to one final conclusion when the child does not admit they are addicted to drugs.

They finally conclude, they have to try the best they can but the offspring has to learn the lesson on their own.

I can tell you emotions are bad.

You will know anger is bad and hate is bad, so you will know emotions can be bad.

But when I suggest all emotions are bad, the confusion kicks in and then one can go no further.

So, I can only do the best I can and be aware you have to learn your lesson.

The part of you that knows emotions can be bad, is your intuition.

The part of you that believes love is good and feeling good is good, is your emotional aspect.

So when that is eliminated all you will have left is your intuition which is you right voice or proper voice.

As long as that emotional aspect throws in it's two cents, there will be confusion.

You may perceive it took me a while to come up with all this.

Well perhaps less than a week based on your time scale.

I don't prepare notes. I don't think about what I am going to say and then say it.

It's all done in real time.

That is a symptom of how extreme the clarity is, once the emotions are silenced.

I am aware no doctor would suggest you block your emotions fully.

I am aware anger management is all about blocking anger emotions.

So people understand some emotions are better off being blocked.

Most people are not fully aware all emotions are better off being blocked.

So they are halfway there, but they are not all the way

there or to the extreme.

So perhaps these words somehow will help some get to the extreme from halfway.

Then the one who does, will read this book and the words will all make perfect sense and they will ask me.

"How on earth did you figure this out?", and I will tell the truth.

This "accident" has enabled me to arrange these words.

Well, who gave these words we call the Bible and Quran and Torah to man?

God manipulated illusions or man to his will.

Man physically is an illusion but the essence of a physical man is Gods essence.

Men at times show their essence. There are many accounts of "enlightened" or "prophets" or "savants"

That is a symptom the essence is strong. Gods essence.

God is outside of the true vacuum.

God has placed his essence, humans, who are spiritual beings, into the true vacuum, to see who the pure essence is and who the flawed essence is. The test is to see if the spiritual beings can understand the physical world is an illusion. If they are able to do this, all that will remain is pure spiritual essence.

That pure spiritual essence will return to God.

That is the "plan".

The wheat will be separated from the chaff.

the seven deadly sins are as follows: *luxuria* **(extravagance, later lust),** *gula* **(gluttony),** *avaritia* **(greed),** *acedia* **(sloth),** *ira* **(wrath),** *invidia* **(envy), and** *superbia* **(pride**

In parallel order to the sins they oppose, the seven holy virtues are chastity, temperance, charity, diligence, patience, kindness, and humility.

The seven deadly sins are emotions or ego , or symptoms of emotions or ego.

The seven holy virtues are the symptoms of one who has no ego or emotion.

"Logical" beings are compelled to suggest words.

These words are their purpose. "Emotional" beings suggest 'Logical" beings are enlightened, but logical beings do not think they are. They are just compelled to "help" but not so they can get something out of it.

They simply just do it. There is no motivation to do it, they just are compelled to do it.

I was compelled to publish this book, it is so. Nothing else is considered.

I was compelled to write these words, they are so. Nothing else is considered.

I perceive I am not doing the compelling, that is so. Nothing else is considered.

"Do not take the word of a blind man, ask questions."

Some people see a glass as half empty, some see a glass as half full and some see no glass at all.

 So perhaps one perceives this, emotional block leading to clarity, cannot be true.

Perhaps that is why I will write more words because I am aware before you read these words when you get to this point in the words you will perceive these words cannot be true.

Lets go back to wikipedias words.I am pleased with the illusion Wikipedia is.

A gamma wave is a pattern of brain waves, associated with perception and consciousness.

What does perception mean to humans?

Let's pretend.

Human beings are special because they have large brains.

Gamma waves are involved in higher mental activity.

Perhaps higher mental activity is relative to perception.

Perhaps perception is relative to ones delusional capacity.

So a small rodent with a tiny brain has different perception than a human with a large brain.

So a tiny rodent with a tiny brain has less perception but not in a bad way, they have less perception so they are less prone to delusional perceptions or illusions.

So humans get in wars over (illusions)nothing and kill each other for (illusions)nothing and attack each other in many ways for (illusions)nothing because their perception is abnormal and makes them think illusions are real. Illusions are not real so the wars and killing are for nothing or over nothing.

Tiny rodents do not kill each other for nothing and get in wars for nothing because their perception is not abnormal or as abnormal as an emotionally based human.

So emotions cause this abnormality in humans but humans can adjust the gamma waves easily by blocking emotions for a period of time so they will lose much of this abnormal perception or ability to believe illusions such as emotional baggage.

So a human has to give up emotions for 3 to 6 months and in return they stop killing each other and harming each other and they will perceive things they will never ever perceive with all those emotions.

Perhaps that is a fair trade off no matter how addicted one is to emotions.

So humans are special because their emotions cause them many delusions and illusions, because they have a large brains.

So humans are special because they can figure out how to block those emotions and adjust their gamma waves so they are not so delusional and prone to believing illusions.

So humans are special because once they adjust their gamma waves and are perceiving properly, they are able to do anything, because they will perceive everything is an illusion and anything is possible if everything is an illusion.

So how did jesus come back from the dead after three days?

Jesus knew there was no death, death was just an illusion.

How did he come back?

He did it because his perception was adjusted because he adjusted his gamma waves and he was able to appear to come back because he was good at using his higher mental activity.

Why did he say "I am with you always even until the end of time."

Because he never left, he reached a state, or was already in that state because he is God, he defeated death by becoming aware or being aware there is no death.

So he is still here because he never left, because he was never here because reality is a true vacuum or nothing or just illusions.

Physical Jesus is an illusion but spiritually God in essence and if an illusion becomes aware it is an illusion it can create any illusion.

Jesus is god. Jesus had a strong essence of God. Jesus was God explaining to humans how they can "see" God better.

If a being is not aware it is an illusion, then that being is limited, they believe the illusion is real so they perceive they cannot do certain things, so they will not be able to do certain things.

"Perception is everything."

Perception is everything because if one has proper perception by adjusting gamma waves they understand everything is a true vacuum or nothing, so then they can do anything because they understand everything is just an illusion.

Do you perceive it took me years to write this book or do you perceive it took me about a week?

So far I've been writing for what you would call three days.

Its wed Jan 21 2009 at 12:56 am, I started writing this
Tuesday Jan 19 2009

The point is, when you are thinking properly you can do
anything.

I am not insulting you by saying you have a sense of time.

I am suggesting you do not have to have, a sense of time.

I am not trying to convince you I am special.

I am trying to convince you, we are special.

I have written things in this book I am self conscious of.

I have written things and misspelled words and misused
commas and just pretty much have no literature mastery.

I am aware I am self conscious of that because I perceive
it matters.

So you see I am still in denial myself, because I have only
been like this since about Nov 1st 2008.

I am perhaps still in shock a bit.

I perceive people will say," oh he writes good words but
he can't spell and use commas so he is stupid."

I am fully aware I am not stupid because stupid is
something, and I am nothing but an illusion so I can not
possibly be stupid.

I am fully aware if I go and correct the grammar in these
words and take out what I feel might hurt others feelings, I
am delusional because I will be submitting, others feelings
are real.

So If no person ever reads this because I did not correct
the grammar properly, that will not matter because

people are just illusions.

So I will not allow one word in this book to be edited to please someone.

I will not allow one word in this book to be edited to please myself.

I refuse to live in denial. I refuse to believe and subscribe to illusions.

I did that for many years and I dam near destroyed myself.

I do not care what anyone thinks, I do not care what anyone says about these words, because they are not fully aware of what I know.

I will not allow delusional people to manipulate me.

I control the illusions because I am aware I am an illusion.

Others bend to the illusions because they perceive the illusions are real.

So you figure out who is in control.

You figure out who is delusional and not thinking properly.

I do not need to figure that out, I am aware of who is in control and I am aware of who is not.

I am not delusional in my beliefs because I am aware everything is an illusion.

So, how did this jesus adjust his gamma waves or how did this jesus condition himself away from emotions or what did jesus tell us was the proper way achieve this "higher mental activity state?"

"turn the other cheek".

Deny emotions, deny ego, then one denies self.

I do not recommend you get slapped for 3 months straight and do not respond to the slaps.

It is perhaps not that difficult, but if one did that, it would work just fine.

Perhaps you should determine what I am before you determine whether my good advice is good advice.

"When the going gets weird, the weird go pro."

You wish I was only pro.

It is to good to be true.

There is no way in hell this information is true.

It's not true because it is to good to be true.

It cannot be this easy.

This guy has a messiah complex.

I am not sure what kind of drugs he is on but I want some.

You need to get some medical help.

Do not try to do what these words suggest.

You need emotions and any doctor will tell you that.

You stay exactly like you are.

You are safe and you are comfortable like you are.

You love your comfort and you love you safety.

You hate change and hate the unknown.

No doctor would ever recommend doing what these words suggest.

You discard these words because you love safety.

You will hate these words so why are you reading them?

You will fear these words so you are better off discarding them.

Don't read anymore, you are only out a few bucks.

You are happy as you are.

You could not be any happier.

You have purpose and you are on top of the world.

You have no purpose and life sucks.

If the author of these words suggests you stop reading perhaps you should do as he suggests.

I am the author and I suggest you just go grab a good classic like Moby Dick or something.

You are not aware of what you are getting into and I am aware of what you are getting into.

You perceive this is a ploy to get you to stop reading these words.

I am saying, this isn't a ploy, this is an honest suggestion, just stop reading these words.

Stop reading these words and do something else. You have all the time in the world to read these words.

You perceive you understand what these words are leading to but I am aware you do not understand what these words will lead to.

Stop reading and call your doctor or counselor and ask them to read these words and ask them to suggest to you if it is okay if you read these words. Then you will be safe.

Better safe than sorry. That's all I am saying.

You are aware words can affect a person. I am aware these words will affect you.

I am suggesting you stop reading these words because they will affect you.

Now your reading more words .

Okay, let me try this.

I don't want you to read these words.

I did not write these words for your pleasure I wrote them to help myself.

So your out a few bucks but now you can stop reading these words.

That's a good trade off. I am suggesting that is a good trade off.

Just let go of the money you spent and then it won't bother you to get rid of these words.

Okay let me try this.

DANGER. DANGER.

Your still reading.

I never planned on anyone reading this far so I am running out of my strategy to get one to stop reading these words.

My strategy to get one to stop reading these words needs adjusting.

Your semi angry or upset now, you want to skip ahead to the good part or you feel this sense of

man what a crap decision it was to acquire these words.

I have no grammar skills and I can't even use a comma properly.

I have to keep everything in short sentence so I don't get confused.

I know less than you know about things.

I am uneducated and I am nothing.

That part up there about , man what a crap decision, I honestly do not know if I should put quotes or capitalize it.

It is sticking out but I don't know what I should do about it.

Did one of your friends talk you into acquiring these words?

They pulled a practical joke on you.

So the joke is over and now you can stop reading these words.

These words are a total waste of time.

Okay, I am going to stop writing and the rest of these pages will be blank, so you can stop reading now.

DO NOT ENTER

That's the universal sign of warning I think, so you should heed it perhaps.

SOS

That's like help, but in this case it's you need help to stop reading these words, so it applies.

Get some kind of drugs and that way you may not remember what you read, if you insist on continuing to read.

You can call one of your friends and tell them "This thing I am reading is so stupid, you should read it."

That way you can stop reading, you need to go give this to them, so they can to see how stupid these words are.

Words are pretty stupid anyway but the arrangement of words in this book are arranged in an especially stupid way.

I am certain that last sentence made perfect sense.

I am not even good at arranging sentences, so why are you reading these poorly arranged sentences.

There are authors who have grasped grammar and comma usage and they want you to read their words.

I don't even want you to read this and I am begging you to stop reading these words and I am trying my best strategy to get you to stop reading these words, and your still reading them.

Your putting my back up against the wall here.

There are some nice video games and movies you could watch and you could go outside and enjoy nature.

Nature is way better than these poorly arranged words, that's a fact.

Nearly every sentence I type I get messages suggesting the sentence I typed has errors.

I am not even sure what I should do.

I am very confused, I am certain I have no grasp on English and I am getting lots of errors when I finish a sentence.

The start of the words is coming up soon.

I have very little time to persuade you so I will try the best I can to stop you.

I am not certain you can read, because I suggested you not read the words, but you still read them.

Perhaps you underestimate what I mean by, you should stop reading these words before they begin.

Perhaps you underestimate me.

If you overestimated me you would listen to my advice to stop reading the words.

Wait...

If you underestimated me you would not be reading the words to begin with.

Wait...

If you underestimate my advice you would underestimate my advice and stop reading, and that means you underestimate me.

If your one of those people who makes up their own mind and doesn't follow the crowd you need to definitely stop reading these words.

If you're a person who likes knowledge and power you need to get rid of these words immediately.

I am just saying if you read these words it is your decision.

If you read these words it is your burden.

Do not like me.

Do not start to like me.

Do not hate me.

Do not start to hate me.

Let me be.

Once, a man found a treasure beyond value.

This man rushed to town to share it with many.

The ones in town were drunk and they were not able to
hold onto the item the man found.

The man became frustrated because few could handle
the treasure in their condition or state.

The man went home and determined if he could not
share the treasure, the treasure would destroy him.

The man went in search of one person who could handle
the treasure, so he would be able to get on with his life.

He realized that search may take his lifetime to achieve.

The man was pleased.

Sometimes one has to let go of what one perceives they should never let go of.

Sometimes the best things are free, but require one to let go of other things, so they can grasp the best thing, that is free.

If one lets go, they will be unsafe until they hit the ground.

I am unable to tell false or claim something that is not the truth.

I can fake it and fake a lie but I am not very good at it.

What you are going to read is all true.

What you are going to read is what truth is like.

Everything in this universe is wisdom or opinion.

Everything is either true or false.

Something happened not long ago and I see wisdom and the rest sticks out like a sore thumb.

It happened recently so I am pleased to say" perhaps" about things I am aware I fully do not understand.

Sometimes I appear arrogant.

Perhaps means maybe.

Try to remember this during these words.

My arrogance is only exceeded by my modesty.

My modesty is only exceeded by wisdom.

When what is false is taken away all that remains is wisdom.

When physicists find the smallest particle they will find empty space.

The wisdom can be painful, wisdom can be pleasing.

What is false is always painful.

Expectations lead to feeling good or feeling bad.

Expectations lead to emotional feelings.

It is difficult for one to fully let go of emotions.

It is more difficult for one to fully let go of certain emotions.

Emotions are addicting, some more than others.

Desires are a symptom of emotions.

Goals and expectations are a symptom of emotional desires.

Depression is a symptom of emotional expectations not met.

Ego is a symptom of emotional expectations met.

One has to let go of the emotional expectation, one is able to fully let go of emotions.

Then one is able to fully let go of most emotions properly.

One in an emotional state is not able to determine if it is proper to let go of all emotions because they are addicted to most emotions and they are reluctant to toss away the drug they crave and have relied on for so long.

It is difficult for an addict to admit their addiction is harming them.

It is more difficult for an addict to actually let go of the addiction.

Letting go of emotions is going to be torture.

Torture leads to the cure.

The cure leads to being pleased.

One who shows weak signs of emotions is fully normal.

One who shows strong signs of emotions is fully abnormal.

One who becomes emotional about reading any of these words is abnormal.

One who hates is abnormal.

One who emotionally loves is abnormal.

One who emotionally loves to hate fully abnormal.

One who hates to emotionally love is fully abnormal.

One who does not hate or emotionally love anything, or anyone, is fully normal.

One that becomes confused reading any of these words is showing strong signs of emotions.

Torture is the cure.

Torture is the way.

Torture is encouraged.

One is pleased to be tortured to be cured.

One is pleased to be cured.

When one is cured, one is pleased.

When the addict lets go of the addiction, the addict is pleased.

Letting go of the addiction is torture.

Letting go of the drug is torture.

Letting go leads to torture.

Letting go is the key to the cure.

Letting go leads to torture and that torture leads to the cure.

One who is worried about what another one says is abnormal.

One who worries about what another one thinks is abnormal.

One who thinks they are not worrying about what others think or say, but are still doing things to please others are fully abnormal.

One who does not worry is normal.

Worry is a symptom of one who is abnormal.

Much worry is a symptom of one who is fully abnormal.

Worry leads to becoming more abnormal.

Worry leads to depression, love and hate.

Worry leads to expectations.

Expectations lead to emotions.

Emotions are abnormal.

Having few emotions is normal.

One who is extremely emotional is fully abnormal.

One who is extremely emotionless is fully normal.

One who is fully normal thinks clearly.

One who is fully abnormal does not think clearly.

Not thinking clearly leads to emotions.

Not thinking clearly leads to improper decisions.

Improper decisions leads to emotions.

Emotions are abnormal.

One who does not think clearly is abnormal.

Not thinking clearly leads to improper decisions.

Improper decisions lead to improper conclusions.

Improper conclusions lead to emotions.

Improper conclusions lead to love and hate.

Improper conclusions lead to wars.

Improper conclusions lead to killing.

Killing other beings is abnormal.

War with other beings is abnormal.

Improper decisions lead to killing other beings.

Improper decisions lead to war with other beings.

Emotion leads to war with other beings.

Killing other beings leads to emotions.

Wars are killing you.

Wars are killing me.

Wars are killing us.

Improper decisions are killing us.

Improper conclusions are killing you.

Abnormality is killing you.

Abnormality is killing us.

Abnormality is emotions.

Emotions are abnormal.

One who suggests war is normal is abnormal.

One who suggests emotions are important is abnormal.

One who suggests emotional love is important is abnormal.

One who suggests hate is important is abnormal.

One who suggests worry is important is abnormal.

One who steals or is greedy is abnormal.

One who desires or lusts is abnormal.

One who craves or covets is abnormal.

One who demands is abnormal.

One who is controlling is abnormal.

One who suggests they are not extremely flawed is abnormal.

One who likes things is abnormal.

One who dislikes things is abnormal.

One who feels much is abnormal.

One who feels little is normal.

One who suggests war is abnormal is normal.

One who suggests emotions are not important is normal.

One who suggests emotional love is not important is normal.

Emotions are abnormal.

One who is abnormal does not think clearly.

One who does not think clearly is abnormal.

One who fears is abnormal.

One who insults others with words is abnormal.

One who attacks others with words is abnormal.

One who is insulted by words is abnormal.

One who is not insulted by words is normal.

One who physically attacks others is abnormal.

One who physically insults others is abnormal.

One who is not insulted by physical attacks is normal.

One who is not insulted by physical insults is normal.

One who thinks clearly is normal.

One who is confused is not thinking clearly.

One who is not thinking clearly is confused.

One who is confused is abnormal.

One who is aware of much is normal.

One who is normal is aware of much.

One who is abnormal is not aware of much.

One who is not aware of much is abnormal.

One who is fully aware is fully normal.

One who has expectations is not aware of much.

One who has no expectations is aware of much.

Emotions are abnormal.

Ego leads to emotions.

Emotions lead to ego.

Ego is abnormal.

Sympathy leads to ego.

Selfishness leads to ego.

Feeling good leads to ego.

Feeling bad leads to emotions.

Expectations lead to ego.

One who is embarrassed is emotional.

Humiliation is normal.

Humiliation blocks emotions.

Humiliation blocks ego.

Meek is normal.

Meek blocks emotions.

Meek blocks ego.

One who is embarrassed by these words in abnormal.

One who is humiliated by these words is normal.

Humble is normal.

One who is angered by these words is abnormal.

One who is humbled by these words is normal.

Emotions are abnormal.

Pleased is normal.

I can see without emotions.

I can think without emotions.

I can see without emotions.

I can think without emotions.

No emotional love, no war, no emotions.

No hate, no emotional love, no emotions.

I can feel without emotions.

I am pleased without emotions.

Pleased is normal without emotions.

One who attacks another is emotional.

One who accepts humiliation after being attacked becomes logical.

One who starts conflict is emotional.

One who avoids conflict is logical.

One who wins a conflict encourages ego.

One who avoids conflict is logical.

One who wins a conflict encourages ego, so loses the conflict of self.

One who loses the conflict encourages logic so wins the conflict of self.

Logic defeats emotions.

Logic defeats emotions without conflict.

Emotion is defeated by logic in conflict.

Emotions are self defeating.

Emotions encourage emotions.

Emotions lead to suffering.

Logic leads to understanding.

Logic leads to strategy.

Emotions lead to confusion.

Confusion leads to emotions.

Strategy is normal.

Confusion is abnormal.

Confusion leads to defeat.

Strategy leads to logic.

Emotions are not logical.

Logic is not emotional.

Confusion is not logical.

Logic is not confusion.

Confusion is not clarity.

Logic is clarity.

Confusion is not understanding.

Understanding is logical.

Anger is confusion.

Anger is not logical.

Greed is confusion.

Money leads to greed.

Food is logical.

Food leads to understanding.

Spite leads to confusion.

If these words are confusing, one is confused.

Confusion is a symptom of emotions.

Emotions is a symptom of confusion.

Love leads to desires.

Desires lead to expectations.

Expectations lead to frustration.

Frustration leads to anger.

Anger leads to hate.

Hate leads to violence.

Violence leads to conflict.

Conflict leads to emotions.

Emotions lead to defeat.

Defeat leads to confusion.

Confusions leads to failure.

Failure leads to frustration.

Frustration leads to anger.

Anger leads to hate.

Hate leads to confusion.

Confusion leads to failure.

Failure leads to failure.

Emotions lead to failure.

Emotions lead to suffering.

Suffering leads to fear.

Fear leads to confusion.

Expect nothing.

Demand nothing.

Get everything.

See everything.

Emotional conditioning leads to clarity.

Clarity leads to understanding.

Understanding leads to imagination.

Imagination leads to strategy.

Strategy leads to Emotional conditioning Strategy.

Emotional Conditioning Strategy leads to logic.

Logic leads to no sense of time.

No Sense of time leads to everything.

No Sense of time is normal.

Sense of time is abnormal.

Logic is normal.

Emotions are abnormal.

Logic leads to understanding.

Emotions lead to confusion.

Understanding leads to reason.

Emotions lead to failure.

Reason leads to purpose.

Failure leads to emotions.

If someone says, Thank you, reply with Thank you.

One will perceive you are gracious.

You will be aware you are conditioning.

If someone demands money, give them more than enough money.

They will perceive you are gracious.

You will be aware you are conditioning.

If someone insults you, allow them to insult you.

They will perceive they have won.

You will be aware you are conditioning.

Their ego will increase.

Your ego will diminish.

Allow others to condition you.

If someone becomes angry with you, ignore them.

Allow them to destroy them self.

Allow your self to condition.

If they become violent, allow them to become violent.

They will lose control, you will gain control.

Clarity is control.

Confusion leads to violence.

 Logic is control.

Emotions lead to confusion.

One who perceives they are something, is nothing.

One who perceives they are nothing, is everything.

One who perceives they are something, is emotional.

One who perceives they are nothing, is logical.

One who perceives they are everything, is abnormal.

One who perceives they are special, is abnormal.

One who perceives they are better, is abnormal.

One who perceives they are abnormal, is special.

One who perceives they are abnormal, is logical.

One who perceives they are abnormal, is normal.

One who submits they are flawed, is normal.

One who submits, is normal.

One who brags, is abnormal.

One who boasts, is abnormal.

One who is proud, is abnormal.

One who underestimates, is abnormal.

One who overestimates, is normal.

One who looks down on others, is abnormal.

One who looks up to others, is normal.

One who settles, is abnormal.

One who doesn't settle, is normal.

One who listens to their intuition, is normal.

One who does not listen to their intuition, is abnormal.

One who thinks two moves ahead has an emotional strategy.

One who thinks as many moves ahead as it takes has a logical strategy.

One who settles easily, is emotional.

One who does not settle easily, is logical.

An understanding being does not need to settle easily.

A confused being desires to settle easily.

Desires lead to expectations.

Expectations lead to emotions.

Emotions lead to easily settling.

Easily settling leads to confusion.

Confusion leads to failure.

An understanding being does not easily settle for failure.

A confused being easily settles for failure.

A logical being does not easily settle for anything.

An emotional being easily settles for everything.

A logical being does not easily settle for limits.

An emotional being easily settles for limits.

A logical being only settles for clarity

An emotional being easily settles for anything.

A logical being only settles for understanding.

An emotional being easily settles for confusion.

A logical being never settles for emotions.

An emotional being easily settles for emotions.

A logical being never settles for hate.

An emotional being easily settles for hate.

A logical being never settles for war.

An emotional being easily settles for war.

A logical being need not settle.

An emotional being needs to settle.

A logical being has confidence.

An emotional being has confusion.

A logical being need not settle for failure.

An emotional being easily settles for failure.

A logical being need not be concerned.

An emotional being needs to be concerned.

A logical being has control.

An emotional being has confusion.

An emotional being has emotions.

A logical being has everything except many emotions.

An emotional being can become a logical being.

A logical being is unable to become an emotional being.

A logical being will welcome torture to stay a logical being.

An emotional being should welcome torture to become a logical being.

Torture is nothing to a logical being.

Torture is everything to an emotional being.

A logical being has no fear.

An emotional being has only fear.

A logical being has no emotional baggage.

An emotional being only has emotional baggage.

A logical being has no cravings.

An emotional being has nothing but cravings.

A logical being has no suffering.

An emotional being has nothing but suffering.

A logical being has no sense of time.

An emotional being has nothing but time.

A logical being has no ego.

An emotional being has nothing but ego.

A logical being ponders self.

An emotional being cares nothing about self.

An emotional being cares only about emotions.

I am aware this will be difficult for you.

I am aware this is difficult for me.

I am aware this is difficult for you.

I am aware of your torture.

I am aware of the torture that awaits you.

I am aware you will win, because I am aware you are capable of doing anything.

I am aware the addiction is powerful.

I am aware the symptoms of the addiction are powerful.

I am aware you desire to resist all of these words.

I am aware you hate these words.

I am aware you perhaps hate me for these words.

I cannot escape my emotions yet I have few emotions.

I am aware emotions are part of self.

I am aware they are able to destroy self.

Emotions are destroying us.

Emotions appear so pleasing yet are so destructive.

Emotions appear as light but lead to darkness.

Logic appears as darkness but leads to light.

These illusions are powerful.

Ones can become convinced emotions are light.

One can become convinced logic is darkness.

One can become convinced confusion is light.

One can become convinced clarity is darkness.

Confusion is darkness.

Clarity is light.

Emotion is darkness.

Logic is light.

Darkness makes light appear to be darkness.

Light reveals darkness to itself.

Darkness is killing you.

Darkness is killing me.

Darkness is killing us.

I am unable to allow darkness to kill me.

I am unable to allow darkness to kill us.

I am aware.

I am aware I am unable.

I am aware I am able.

I am aware I am able to stop darkness from killing me.

I am aware I am able to stop darkness from killing us.

I do not underestimate darkness.

I do not underestimate the torture I endure.

I do not underestimate the torture awareness is.

A logical being is aware everyone is important.

An emotional being see's few as important.

A logical being is aware self is important.

A logical being perceives self is not important.

An emotional being is aware self is not important.

An emotional being perceives self is important.

One who understands they are nothing, understands everything.

One who understands they are everything, understands nothing.

One who ponders being everything, ponders nothing.

One who ponders being nothing, ponders everything.

Some are able to see, but many are unable to see they are able to see.

They underestimate their self.

Underestimating ones self is a symptom of confusion.

Confusion is a symptom of emotions.

Understanding ones self is nothing, conditions away from emotions.

Conditioning away from emotions encourages logic.

Logic encourages clarity.

Clarity encourages understanding.

Understanding encourages further conditioning away from emotions.

I am aware many hear, but do not understand.

I am aware many see, but do not understand.

I am aware all are able to see. I am aware all are able to understand.

I am aware many are unable to understand, they are able to see.

Conditioning away from emotions enables one to see.

Conditioning away from emotions enables clarity.

Clarity enables one to understand they are able to see.

Understanding one is able to see, encourages further conditioning away from emotions.

An emotional being seeks acceptance.

A logical being avoids emotional feelings.

An emotional being seeks popularity.

A logical being avoids emotional desires.

An emotional being seeks material wealth.

A logical being seeks understanding and clarity.

An emotional being seeks emotions.

A logical being seeks to condition away from emotions.

No sense of time is normal.

An emotional being does not understand there is no time.

An emotional being does not see there is no time.

An emotional being does not believe there is no time.

An emotional being is confused.

Emotions lead to confusion.

Confusion leads to improper decisions.

Improper decisions lead to feelings of frustration and failure.

Feelings of frustration and failure lead to anger and bitterness.

Feelings of success encourage ego and emotions.

Ego and emotions lead to emotions and confusion.

Emotions leading to further emotions, is an infinite cycle.

Clarity leading to further clarity, is an infinite cycle.

An emotional being is trapped in an infinite cycle of emotions.

A logical being is pleased with the infinite cycle of logic.

An emotional being is tortured in an infinite cycle of confusion.

A logical being is pleased in an infinite cycle of understanding.

I perceive emotions are pleasing, I am aware emotions are darkness.

I perceive emotions are light, I am aware emotions are killing us.

I perceive I desire to condition away from emotions, I am aware desire is and emotional feeling.

I perceive the harder I try to avoid emotions the more emotional I feel.

I perceive the more emotion I feel the harder I must try to condition away from emotions.

This is an infinite cycle.

Emotions cannot be eliminated, only silenced.

Logic cannot be eliminated, only encouraged.

If one is encouraging emotion they are silencing logic.

If one is silencing emotions they are encouraging logic.

If one is encouraging emotions they are encouraging confusion.

If one is encouraging logic they are encouraging clarity.

An emotional being perceives a logical being has great clarity.

A logical being perceives they have slight clarity.

A logical being perceives and emotional being is confused.

An emotional being perceives they have clarity.

An emotional being perceives their perception is normal.

A logical being perceives an emotional beings perception is abnormal.

A logical being perceives no sense of time.

No sense of time is relative to ones perception.

Sense of time is relative to ones perception.

Clarity is relative to ones perception.

Gamma waves in the brain influence ones perception.

Gamma waves in the brain are influenced by emotions.

Gamma waves can be controlled by conditioning away from emotions.

Gamma waves can be controlled by conditioning away from logic.

Gamma waves control ones perception of time.

Gamma waves control ones perception of physical pain.

Gamma waves control ones perception of mental pain.

I perceive these words make sense, I am aware an emotional being will perhaps be confused by these words in this book.

I perceive this perception self is due to gamma waves In the brain.

I perceive the awareness is a self, unrelated to perception self.

This awareness self is observing the perception self.

Awareness self is intuition.

Emotional beings have intuition.

Logical beings have intuition.

Logical beings have a more pronounced intuition.

Gamma waves influence perception, and perception influences intuition, perhaps.

When one's intuition warns them of a bad situation it is perhaps unrelated to ones perception.

This intuition self is mysterious.

This awareness self is mysterious.

This perception self is explainable and relates to gamma waves in the brain.

No sense of time is explainable and relates to gamma waves in the brain.

Sense of time is explainable and relates to gamma waves in the brain.

This is pleasing because it eliminates supernatural explanations.

It is pleasing because it is explainable. It is understandable.

This intuition self or awareness self is not explainable and perhaps is supernatural.

Supernatural relates to things that are not scientifically explainable.

Things not scientifically explainable are left to interpretation.

Interpretations or opinions cause confusion.

Confusion may lead to emotional feelings such as frustration and anger.

Frustration and anger may lead to feelings of failure or suffering.

Failure and suffering may lead to feelings of inadequacies.

Inadequacies lead to one becoming humbled or meek.

When one is humbled or meek , this state encourages logic.

The more humbled one becomes the more logical one becomes.

The more logical one becomes the more one is humbled.

The more one understands, the more one understands, they understand little.

This leads to one becoming more humble.

A logical being is aware of these cycles of infinity in nearly everything.

A logical being perceives these cycles of infinity in nearly everything.

These cycles of infinity are symptoms of a fact.

An emotional being may not perceive what these words are relating to.

An emotional being perhaps is becoming aware of what these words are leading to.

An emotional being will come to a crossroad where they will have a choice.

They can retreat into their safe and pleasing confusion.

They can let go of safety and embrace the unknown and the impossible.

Their true self will be revealed to them alone.

They will let go and forge on with courage or they will shrink at impossibilities.

They will grow up or they will remain as they are.

They will understand or they will never understand.

They will understand what they are or they will live in denial forever.

They will hold onto pleasing emotions or embrace uncertain logic.

They will choose sweet darkness or bitter light.

They will choose comfort or they will choose torture.

If they choose comfort they will think they have won, when they have lost.

If they choose torture they will think they have lost, when they have won.

"One who loses themselves, will find them self."

"I must be willing to give up what I am in order to become what I will be."

                    ***Einstein**

One who lets go of emotions, will discover who they are.

From the darkness will emerge light.

Clarity will emerge from confusion.

An emotional being is no different than a logical being because both are beings.

An emotional being differs from a logical being only in gamma waves.

An emotional being differs from a logical being only in perception.

Beings are exactly the same, beings are totally different.

Beings are beings, beings gamma waves are different.

Gamma waves are the only difference in beings.

Gamma waves are scientifically valid.

An emotional being is not worse and is not better than a logical being.

A logical being is not worse and is not better than an emotional being.

Both logical and emotional beings are still beings.

Logical beings are aware they are normal.

Logical beings are aware emotional beings are emotionally abnormal.

Logical beings are pleased if they can humbly suggest words to emotional beings.

Logical beings are not out to prove themselves because they are aware of what they are.

They do not need to prove it to others because they have few emotions or ego.

They are compelled to suggest words.

They are not arrogant in their words they are just compelled to suggest words.

They are aware they are flawed, they are aware they have burdens.

They are mindful of their impossible task, they are mindful they cannot fail in that task.

They perceive they are something else, they are aware they are nothing.

The logical being is conflicted with contradictions.

The logical being is conflicted with infinite cycles.

The more logical they become the more confusion arises.

The more confusion arises the more logical they are compelled to become.

The LB is mindful that they may revert back to the emotional state.

That is their hell, that is their nightmare. They will sacrifice everything to avoid that hell.

They are aware of how they used to be and their core being is mindful , hell may return.

They are compelled for logic and understanding, but they are uncertain about hell returning.

They over compensate, this reverting back to an emotional state is the evil one.

They fear nothing except how they used to be , because they are fully aware of how they used to be.

The LB is aware they are flawed because they are aware they are unable to guarantee they will never revert back to that emotional state.

The emotional being perceives the LB is exceptional but the logical being is aware they are flawed, because they cannot guarantee they will never revert back to the emotional state.

The LB has to submit their logic cannot overcome this possibility that they may revert back to the emotional state, so they are stuck in this over compensating, conditioning away from emotions state.

The logical being is aware they are never safe. There is no safety. There is no comfort. It can all come crashing down any moment.

To an EB the LB appears exceptional but at the core of LB's being they are aware the emotional state can return.

They are aware they are nothing if they cannot guarantee this emotional state will never return.

They are humbled because they are aware even though

they are exceptional in appearance they are flawed to the core.

One flaw, means flawed.

The logical being is aware they are flawed.

That encourages them to condition further from emotions.

That enables them to go further into logic.

That further modifies the gamma waves.

That further changes their perception.

That perception change enables them more clarity.

That further clarity enables them to understand more.

That further understanding leads them to understand they are flawed more clearly.

That is an infinite cycle.

These infinite cycles are also a symptom they are flawed.

The infinite cycles they perceive everywhere are indication they are flawed.

So they seek further clarity but full clarity is not possible.

Emotions are part of a being, they cannot be eliminated.

As the flaws increase, the conditioning away from emotions increases, and the clarity increases, which reveals further flaws.

There is no escape from the infinite cycles, so a logical being must allow some infinite cycles to be.

If a logical being cannot let go of some logical infinite cycles they will harm them self.

If an emotional being cannot let go of emotional infinite cycles they will harm them self.

A logical being who lets go of some logical infinite cycles conditions away from emotions.

An emotional being who lets go of some emotional infinite cycles conditions away from emotions.

Either being, who does not learn to let go, gets trapped in the infinite cycles and harms them self.

I am not aware of thinking ahead.

I am not aware of planning out what I am going to say.

I perceive these words are making a point.

I am aware these words will have the effect they always have on EB's.

I am in the present.

One sentence leads to another.

One thing leads to another.

There is no better time than the present.

I have no expectations because I am in the present.

I am aware I used to have past and future thoughts but I can no longer relate to what that feeling is like.

I can try to fake it but I fail.

I try to be humble but I come off sounding arrogant.

I try to tell the truth as I see it but emotional beings perceive I tell lies.

Some emotional beings see glimmers of truth in these words.

Some emotional beings are entertained by these words.

Some emotional beings are angered by these words.

Some emotional beings see intelligence in these words.

Some emotional beings see wisdom in these words.

Some EB's suggest I should be a prophet.

Some EB's suggest I should be a saint.

Some EB's suggest I am enlightened.

Some EB's suggest I should be a Buddha, because of my words.

Some psychologists suggest I should be a patient, because of my symptoms.

The EEG machine is the one I trust because a machine is able to determine what kind of a machine I am.

The EEG machine tells the truth.

The EEG machine has no emotions, it is only capable of truth.

It does one thing and it does it well.

It has no expectations.

It is not concerned with what others think about its results.

It does what it does and it moves onto the next task.

The tasks are infinite.

The machine is pleased with infinity.

Without infinity there is an end.

An end is a limit.

Infinity is limitless.

Infinity is a symptom of a fact.

The MRI machine suggests my brain is fully healthy.

The EEG machine suggests my brain waves are fully healthy.

My gamma waves are at the high end of the normal limits, but that is all.

Is any Doctor going to know was is healthy, and what is not healthy, better than a machine?

I trust the machine because the machine is not capable of delusions and ego and emotions.

Conditioning is going to change how your brain functions.

It's permanent.

Some EB's will suggest its dangerous or unhealthy.

Some EB's will suggest powerful drugs are healthy but conditioning is unhealthy.

Some EB's will suggest powerful drugs are a cure but conditioning is unhealthy.

Do you think they want you to stop taking the depression

drugs they make a living off of prescribing to you?

Do you think they will admit they need you to make money?

If anyone no matter who they are suggests this conditioning is unhealthy, you ask them one question.

Do you have a sense of time?

If they say," Yes". They do not know what they are talking about.

If they have not experienced it, they are unable to talk factually about it, ever.

It does not matter who they think they are.

Change, denotes unknown.

You get used to no sense of time just as you are used to a sense of time.

You get used to having few emotions just like you are used to having many emotions.

You're a human being and your main attribute is adaptability.

You will do just fine.

You will know when it happens and it is like the" ah ha" sensation.

When someone tells you a riddle and you don't get it and they tell you the answer and you say

"Wow that was so easy, and I made it so hard."

That is when it has happened.

It is subtle, yet when this shift from EB to LB happens you get that "ah ha" sensation.

That's when everything starts to make sense.

I do not mean some things, I mean everything.

This is a decision for you, about you.

This is the most important decision you will ever make in your life, period.

You know what the decision is, you know what your choices are.

For once in your life you get to make a very important decision.

Everything rests on your decision. Everything depends on your decision.

There is no one there to help you make this decision. You are on your own.

You have to rely on your self.

If you hate yourself you won't trust your self.

If you love yourself you won't want to let go of your self.

Now you are aware of why it is the most important decision you will ever make in your life.

Anything that makes you feel must be denied, period.

If you want to go buy something you like or want, do not do it.

If someone insults you and you want to make a clever comeback do not do it.

If you want to sound intelligent, do not do it.

If you want to get the last word in, do not do it.

If you want to buy someone a gift, do not do it.

If you want to compliment someone, do not do it.

If you want to eat some food you crave, do not do it.

If you start to think you are good, do not think that.

If you want to be kind, do not be kind.

If you want to hurt someone, do not hurt someone.

If someone gives you anything, accept it but when you get home throw it away or throw it in a closest and do not acknowledge it.

Avoid money with all of your heart, only use money if you have to.

Anger management goes like this.

You detect when your getting upset and you stop and count to 10 until that anger passes.

You apply that to every single emotion or feeling you have.

Should take about three to six months or less.

It's not about money or someone teaching you directions.

It is all about you.

The best things in life are free.

The best thing you will ever do in your life is to condition yourself away from emotions.

It is free to do.

You are free to do it.

No one can stop you, they can only confuse you and make you hesitate, and make you doubt yourself.

So do you know better or does someone who doesn't know much know better?

Do you trust yourself over everyone else?

If you do not, you underestimate yourself, your not in communication with yourself.

You deny yourself.

You need to get used to reality quickly.

You are an important being. You are.

You are capable of making the most important decision you will ever make, by yourself.

Others may have suggested or insinuated you are not an important being, but they do not know much.

If someone does not know you are an important being, they know nothing.

I do not care who they think they are, they are confused.

If someone suggests you are not capable of making this decision, they know nothing.

Avoid them, they are confused.

They are an EB and they think they are normal.

They will yell at you and insult you and harm you and then suggest they are normal.

They will say take these mind altering drugs and take them when I suggest you should.

They will say they are normal and they will say I am abnormal.

I am saying they are abnormal and I am normal.

They will say a sense of time is normal and I am saying a sense of time is abnormal.

I am not asking you to take mind altering drugs.

I am not asking you to do anything.

I am aware you are an important being and can decide everything for yourself.

You can decide to help yourself and I am aware you are capable of making that decision by yourself.

So you can become aware of what you are.

I am fully aware of your potential.

I am unable to underestimate your potential.

You make this choice yourself because your self is who you are stuck with.

Perhaps it is wise to get to know your self a bit.

This method will help you know your self a bit.

There are moments you get glimpses of who you are but being an EB means that's all you get are glimpses.

The emotions are blocking your view so you get a foggy glimpse.

So the adjusted gamma waves clears the window and you get the full glimpse.

Then nothing will be the same again.

You do not need anyone else but you.

You do not need anything but you.

EB's try to feel important with money and surgery and drugs and diets and clothes.

They are trapped in this infinite cycle of satisfaction or justification of themselves.

They say, "Look at my new things.", they are saying to themselves," I am an important being aren't I?"

They perceive they are not and important being.

 They try to be an important being because they perceive they are not an important being.

I am not pleased with you because I am aware of what you are going through and it is killing me.

I don't write these words to help you.

I am only suggesting you can help your self.

If you help yourself, I won't have to be aware of what you are doing to yourself.

I am not pleased to be aware of what you are doing to your self, I am only human.

I am compelled to write these words because the more aware I become, the more emotional pain I feel , the more emotions I feel, and the further I get away from logic.

I am not compelled to explain how much it hurts me to you, I am fully certain you are unable to understand what higher torture is and what higher pain is due to your emotional state.

 You wear your emotions on your sleeve.

An EB is unable to understand the level a LB has to get to in awareness to tear up.

An LB thinks in real time. They speak as they go.

There is no thinking about what they are going to say before they say it.

They go from one sentence to the next.

They go from one conclusion to the next.

They sometimes go places they didn't expect in their conclusions.

The emotions that happen don't last.

In general LB's have a great sense of humor and appear "enlightened" in what they say.

Laughter is a symptom of clarity.

There is lots of laugher.

When someone tells you the answer to the riddle you couldn't get, you laugh and say that was so simple.

That's the laughter. The laughter of understanding.

It's not a laughter of hate or a laughter at another's expense.

It is real laughter.

I am aware of much.

I am a male so I am not aware of what a female experiences during pregnancy.

I can try to imagine but I will never know for sure, ever.

This fetus is aware of it's mother.

It is aware the mother is the most important being it has ever known.

It knows nothing but that.

Everything else is nothing compared to that mother the fetus is aware of.

The mother is aware that fetus is an important being.

In some cases the mother may attempt to deny that but that is because the mother is trying to talk

 herself out of what she is aware of.

A mother who decides on an abortion is not convincing others her decision is right, she is only attempting to convince herself the decision is right, to abort the fetus.

The mother who knows she is carrying an important being, convinces herself she should abort that important being because she does not have enough money to justify that important being.

I perceive I cannot make you change, but I am aware I will make you change.

I am pleased with my awareness.

You are changed.

It is abnormal for one to deny reality.

It is abnormal for one to deny what they know is true.

This is relative to this whole conditioning thing.

EB's are not sick in the sense of illness.

EB's are sick in the sense of perception.

They suggest they love others but they gladly insult others.

They suggest they want to kill others so there will be peace.

They suggest they want to be healthy but they do things that are not healthy.

They suggest one should treat everyone fairly but they do not treat everyone fairly.

They suggest they only want to help you but they end up hurting you.

They suggest they want to love you but they end up hating you.

Even the greatest EB's hate something or has some underlying motive.

The EB's who suggest they are righteous end up being the least righteous.

The EB who suggests they are not worthy are most worthy.

I will not allow myself to hold onto this information.

I will not love it, I will let go of it.

It will not destroy me because I will let go of it.

I am very aware of what this information is and this conditioning will lead to.

I am very aware of how powerful this conditioning is relative to improving things.

I have to let go of it swiftly.

I will end this book with these words.

I will be mindful of these words during the next book.

I will attempt to be mindful of these words in all other books I will write.

The book of genesis, the first sentence says, God created the heavens and the earth.

That was a test.

If one understands that , they will submit to something greater than themselves.

This is a form of ego conditioning.

If one reads any further in the book past that first sentence, they are not following that first sentence.

They are not submitting fully to one who is greater. So they fail the test.

Submitting does not mean think. It does not mean ask questions. It does not mean give opinions.

It means do nothing but mentally submit.

Do nothing but mentally submit to yourself that you are not that important.

That is the ultimate emotional conditioning, nothing is more extreme.

Buddha suggested blocking ones ego and emotions will lead to enlightenment or clarity.

Abraham was asked to show he could let go of his love for Isaac when he was asked to kill Isaac.

Jesus suggested one should turn the other cheek so one

can become meek.

Mohammed suggested one should submit and submission is a form of humiliation or blocking ego.

If the conditioning that is suggested in this book is wisdom, then all of these beings who suggested this emotional conditioning before me, are wise.

Just listen to your intuition and ignore your emotional aspect.

I am unable to fail in my strategy.

I am unable to allow an illusion to go on thinking it is real.

My strategy will not fail because my strategy is not real.

My strategy will not fail because failure is not real.

My strategy has no limits.

The more it costs me to continue my strategy, the more pleased I am to let go of the illusion, money.

The more clarity I gain by letting go of the illusions the better my strategy becomes.

That is why this book is an experiment.

What I learn from this book will enable me to adjust strategy for the next book.

Being recognized by an important being is a reward beyond value.

An important being, that recognizes they are just a being, is a being beyond value.

You are a being beyond value, I recognize it, and I am humbly suggesting you can recognize it.

There is only being and becoming.

I am not about limits.

I am not about walls.

I am not about isolation.

I am not about emotions.

I am not about halfway.

I am not about safety.

I am a being that is free.

I am pleased about fully letting go, into infinity.

I am being.

The illusions are very strong illusions for some.

A drug addict is convinced their addiction is very strong and hard to break.

A person who is not addicted to drugs has no problem with drugs, they have no desire and no inclination to use drugs.

So the drug addict is in a state of being convinced drugs are very powerful or have a control over him.

But the non drug addict is aware drugs have no control over themselves.

Both people can't be right at the same time.

Some are convinced emotions are required, or one cannot function in the absence of emotions, or one would be very confused in the absence of emotions.

Some are convinced they are able to function much better in the absence of emotions and are way less confused in the absence of emotions.

Both people cannot be right at the same time.

If love is good for a person then hate is good for a person.

If feeling good is good for a person, than feeling bad is good for a person.

If emotions are good for a person, then all emotions are good for a person.

If all emotions are good for a person, then having infinite emotions is very good for a person.

If having emotions is good for a person, than being an emotional wreck is very good for a person.

If ego is good for a person, then having infinite ego is very good for a person.

I am certain this concept of a two way street , relating to ego and emotions, is a false concept..

If you have a harmony or 50/50 attitude relating to emotions and ego you are doomed, i am certain of that.

You need to determine, if you are even able to determine who I am, before you determine you are able to determine, if the wisdom in this book is relative to you.

If I was able to feel the emotion, "care about what others think about the sentences you type in this book" to strongly, It would lead to the emotion, "delete the sentences you perceive may affect how people will feel."

That would lead me to delete every sentence in this book.

Then there would be no sentences and no book.

Then I would have destroyed what I perceive are important sentences, because I cared what others think about the sentences I perceived were important sentences.

I have not allowed that emotional illusion "care about what others think about the sentences you type in this book" to destroy the sentences I perceive are important sentences.

This book is proof of that.

The spirit of this book is wisdom or foolishness. Your spirit will determine that.

I am fully certain you should determine if you are able to determine who I am, so that you will be able to attempt to determine who I am, then you will be able to determine if you can determine you can determine the wisdom in this book, is wisdom, but only if your attempt to determine who I am is a proper determination and not an improper determination.

Torture leads to the cure.

Perhaps it is wise not to take the word of a blind man, such as I.

Your guess is as good as mine.

Perhaps.